EDUCATION IN A COMPETITIVE AND GLOBALIZING WORLD

CAPACITY BUILDING FOR ENVIRONMENT LEARNING AND SUSTAINABLE LIVING: ENVIRONMENTAL MANAGEMENT SYSTEMS IN SCHOOLS IN SOUTH AFRICA

Education in a Competitive and Globalizing World

Additional books in this series can be found on Nova's website under the Series tab.

EDUCATION IN A COMPETITIVE AND GLOBALIZING WORLD

CAPACITY BUILDING FOR ENVIRONMENT LEARNING AND SUSTAINABLE LIVING: ENVIRONMENTAL MANAGEMENT SYSTEMS IN SCHOOLS IN SOUTH AFRICA

LUC HENS
TORSTEN WIEDEMANN
SCHALK RAATH
PAUL RENDERS
ERIC CRAENHALS
AND
BARRY RICHTER

Nova Science Publishers, Inc.
New York

For permission to use material from this book please contact us:
Telephone 631-231-7269; Fax 631-231-8175
Web Site: http://www.novapublishers.com

LIBRARY OF CONGRESS CATALOGING-IN-PUBLICATION DATA

Capacity building for environment learning and sustainable living : environmental management systems in schools in South Africa / Luc Hens ... [et al.].
p. cm.
Includes index.
ISBN 978-1-61209-333-8 (softcover)
1. Environmental management--South Africa. 2. School management and organization--South Africa. 3. Environmental education--South Africa. 4. Elementary schools--Environmental aspects--South Africa. I. Hens, Luc, 1951-
GE320.S6C37 2010
333.720968--dc22

2010048338

Published by Nova Science Publishers, Inc. † New York

CONTENTS

Preface		vii
Chapter 1	Introduction	1
Chapter 2	Project History	3
Chapter 3	Vision	5
Chapter 4	Strategy	7
Chapter 5	Characteristics of the EMS	9
Chapter 6	Implementation	13
Chapter 7	Evaluation of the EMS	29
Chapter 8	Conclusion	47
Acknowledgments		49
References		51
Index		53

PREFACE

For eight years (2003–2010) primary schools in South Africa have been involved in a project to implement Environmental Management systems (EMS) into school management and to reduce the school's environmental impact by introducing an environmental care programme.

After the EMS was implemented and the environment was integrated in the curriculum, activities in the monitored school were measured. Data were collected, based on detailed questionnaires, related to four environmental aspects: water, waste, energy and greening and to three managerial aspects: environmental management; integration of environment in the curriculum; and attitude of learners, teachers and staff-members. The questionnaire results were complemented with data of a "ground truth check" by an independent expert. At the beginning of the project, 50% of the schools performed well on water-related environmental actions. Two years later this figure was raised to 76%. For waste-related activities the improvement was even stronger: from 50% to 100%. The environmental performances of the schools also improved for greening related actions, from 50% at the start of the project to 64% two years later. Only energy-related activities did not improve significantly, with only 24% of all schools performing well at the end of the survey-period.

The monitoring results show the main parameters, which improved in the environmental performance of the schools. These results can be used to improve the process of EMS implementation in the future.

This chapter describes the setup of the EMS and the guidelines for schools to implement environmental care and environmental management in the school's curriculum and management. Monitoring results of environmental care are presented and the correlation analyses between the different managerial aspects on the one hand and the environmental performances on the other hand are discussed.

This chapter is valuable for researchers, governments, educators and other professionals. The results draw attention to the advantages and possibilities of the implementation of EMS at schools. This opens opportunities for further research on how to optimize the operation of an EMS in schools and how to integrate environmental issues in school curricula.

Chapter 1

INTRODUCTION

Most environmentalists agree that if present trends of population growth, pollution and ecological instability will continue, the planet earth's life support system will be prone to collapse. Responsible educators should address this fact in the education of future citizens (Raath et al., 2009, p.6).

Schools as centres of education have to tackle environmental issues in a positive way. Using the learners' experiences and involving them in searching for solutions towards more sustainable ways of living, they will realize their responsibilities and capabilities to deal with environmental problems.

Schools as organizations provide a service to their learners. During the provision of this service, resources (gasoline, electricity, water, paper, etc.) are consumed. During consumption, waste is produced, which might have a negative impact on the environment. To deal with the waste stream and the responsible use of resources, it is suggested that the school makes use of an Environmental Management System (EMS) that is integrated into the management system the school uses.

An EMS cannot only be used as a tool to manage the environmental performance of the school as an organization. At the same time, it offers opportunities for environmental learning.

An environmental management system ensures that the environment is taken into account in all management decisions. When implemented in a school, the environmental management system allows the school to do the following:

- Provide insight into the impact of the school on the environment,
- Show how the school can reduce its impact on the environment,

- Provide options for optimal management of resources,
- Create behavioural changes in the school,
- Reduce school expenditure and
- Promote environmental learning in an integrated way

(Raath et al., 2009, p.8).

For eight years (2003–2010) primary schools in South Africa have been involved in a project to implement EMS in the school management and to reduce the school's environmental impact and to support environmental learning.

This chapter provides insight into the vision, planning and practical aspects of the implementation of an EMS in 39 primary schools in South Africa. The main monitoring results document the impact of the projects.

Chapter 2

PROJECT HISTORY

Capacity building for an environmental learning programme was advocated by the Plan of Implementation of the WSSD in Johannesburg in 2002 (Hens and Nath, 2003).

During the period 2003–2010 the environment and education departments of the Flemish Community of Belgium funded three successive projects on environmental care in primary schools in South Africa:

1) "Education for the environment: an eco-schools partnership project" (2003–2005). This was a pilot project to develop the necessary materials to manage an EMS. The system was implemented in six schools. An interesting aspect of this project was that it widened the scope from environmental targets to sustainable development (http://www.vub.ac.be/MEKO/projects/safrica/newslet2.doc).
2) "Building capacity for sustainable living. Implementation of environmental management in primary schools in South Africa" (2006–2008). This project introduced EMS in 39 primary schools in Gauteng North and Limpopo. The project provided training and logistic support to build environmental targets in a cross- sectional way into the curriculum. It had an outspoken component of monitoring the results of the use of EMS (http://www.vub.ac.be/MEKO/projects/safrica/southafr.html).
3) "Educational support to develop environmental management in primary schools in South Africa". Since 2009, 60 schools in South Africa (Limpopo, Gauteng North, Freestate and NW Province) have been involved in the project

(http://www.vub.ac.be/MEKO/projects/safrica/Project2009.htm).

Chapter 3

Vision

The vision of the project is to commit schools to the protection, conservation and enhancement of the environment and to support the development of a system that will result in the responsible use of resources and the prevention of damage to the environment.

The main aim is to support schools in elaborating projects focusing on the knowledge and skills about the surrounding environment and how to treat the environment in a sustainable way.

Chapter 4

STRATEGY

The project focuses on four areas of a primary importance for sustainable development in South Africa. These are: water, waste, energy and greening. The relevance of the choice of energy has recently been demonstrated during the electricity crisis the country faced during the first months of 2008. Furthermore, in all 4 areas (water, waste, energy and greening) the schools as organisations have an impact on the environment.

Rationale of the operations:

- An environmental management system for a school must be designed down from the Senior School Management level to filter into all the operational aspects of the school, such as financial management, management of facilities and curriculum management.
- The system is dependent on a well developed network of relationships that includes all members of the community.
- Thorough planning and teamwork are keys to effective environmental management. This entails that the objectives and targets set for the environmental management system of the whole school must be known and adhered to by everybody involved.

Chapter 5

CHARACTERISTICS OF THE EMS

The two main characteristics of the EMS are: interdisciplinary and participation

1. INTERDISCIPLINARY: THE EMS IS LINKED TO ALL LEARNING AREAS

"An EMS in a school is a systematic, coherent set of measures and provisions intended to: quantify, prevent and, where possible, limit the amount of pollution generated by the school" (Van Volsem et al., 1997, p.47).

The word system refers to the integrated aspects of an organization. When an EMS is implemented at a school, it ensures that the environment is taken into account in the management decisions of the school, as well as in decisions regarding the implementation of the curriculum. The EMS should

- provide insight in the school's real impact on the environment,
- show how the school can reduce its impact on the environment,
- identify aspects that could have an impact on the environment,
- involve all the stakeholders of the school and develop options for the optimal management of resources,
- initiate behavioural changes at the school,
- reduce school expenditure on environmental resources.

(Raath et al., 2004, p.6)

There are three aspects of an EMS in primary schools:

a) Environmental learning,
b) Managerial aspects for the implementation of environmental management,
c) Environmental care on subjects where schools as organisations have an impact on the environment.

(Hens in: http://www.vub.ac.be/MEKO/projects/safrica/newslet2.doc, p.1)

- For example "energy use at home" can be linked to natural sciences and technology.
- The explanation of the origin of water and how it passes through the water cycle can be integrated in technology, social sciences and natural sciences.
- The themes "waste production" and "waste management" can be linked to social sciences and life orientation.
- Planting and taking care of trees on the school ground can be implemented in technology and natural sciences.

(Raath et al., 2009).

2. Participation: The EMS Involves All Stakeholders, Not Only the School but also the Community Is Involved

When a school decides to work towards sustainable living practices, it depends on a well-developed network of relationships that includes all members of the community:

- Learners,
- Headmasters and persons responsible for the organisation,
- Teachers,
- Parents,
- School administration and
- Other members of the school community.

As learners are the majority in the school they should be actively engaged in solving (environmental) problems. Teachers need to create and facilitate planned activities for learners to be actively involved in problem solving.

Lessons should be learner-focused and not teacher-focused. Methods such as debates, field work and demonstrations should be used by teachers in a learner-centred way to enhance learner participation.

Whether keeping a school garden, protecting the habitat of an endangered species, or designing a recycling programme, pupils learn best from active engagement in which their actions count and have meaning for them. The school's sustainability projects should therefore be selected by communities and focus on themes that are important and meaningful. In this way, the learners will recognize that knowledge is essential to what they care about. They will also learn that they can make a difference (especially towards the protection of the environment) with their involvement, which is a foundation for a responsible, active citizenship.

Teachers need to prepare their environmental learning activities/ lessons in a way that they support the overarching EMS of the school. The whole school (management, teachers and learners) will collaborate to achieve specific objectives and targets that are ımportant to them.

The EMS aims at develop knowledge, skills and responsibility. It introduces environmental care and environmental management.

To achieve this, the schools involved in the project sign an “environmental declaration” (see box text 1).

Chapter 6

IMPLEMENTATION

6.1. ENVIRONMENTAL CARE AND EMS – STEP-BY-STEP PLAN

The following steps are suggested to schools to plan, organize and communicate the EMS. These steps are not a recipe, but only guidelines that can be used and adapted to the unique circumstance of schools:

- Step 1 - School commitment
- Step 2 - Involvement of the community
- Step 3 - Environmental questioning
- Step 4 - Identify a theme
- Step 5 - Develop an action plan
- Step 6 - Implement the action plan on all levels
- Step 7 - Self evaluation

Step 1 - School Commitment

South Africa recently implemented a new curriculum which foresees that the environment has to be integrated in all the learning areas. Environmental care and management are therefore prescribed by the curriculum (Revised National Curriculum Statement (RNCS) (DoE, 2002, p.8)).

Experiences show that signing the school commitment is a crucial first step that cannot be overlooked. The senior management of the school must be committed to develop and maintain an environmental management system (EMS) in the school.

A written commitment must be drawn up, where the school confirms its intention to work towards environmental sustainable living.

We intend to:
• develop a framework for setting and reviewing environmental objectives and targets; • document, implement, maintain and communicate the EMS to all teachers, parents and learners; • annually review the system to ensure continual improvement ; • persistently strive towards prevention of negative impacts on the environment; • comply with relevant environmental legislation and regulations, and with other requirements to which the school subscribes; • integrate sustainable living practises in the learning programs of the learners' curriculum; • actively work towards the development of environmental knowledge, skills and positive attitudes.

Raath et al., 2009.

Box 1. Example of an environmental commitment for a school.

This will then serve as a communication and marketing tool to be displayed in the staff room, classrooms and administration offices so that everyone remains aware and involved in the project.

Step 2 - Involvement of the Stakeholders

The broader school community must be invited to become involved in the development of a whole school approach for education towards sustainable living.

An outcome of the community participation process should be the identification of school members that will serve on an environmental committee (EC). The EC must represent learners, teachers and school community members. It can be complemented with a representative of the parents and a representative of the neighbourhood around the school. The EC drives the EMS. Meetings must be scheduled on a regular basis, work must be allocated, and a year program must be worked out.

The EC, in consultation with the school management, should ideally appoint an enthusiastic teacher to act as the coordinator of the environmental committee. This person will be develop and implement the environmental management system (EMS). She or he is appointed by the EC on the basis of a documented advice of the school principal. The coordinator will not only guide the implementation of the EMS in the school, but is also responsible for the networking with and among the stakeholders, mainly through the EC. The environmental coordinator works in close collaboration with the school principal and the governing body. She or he heads a team that implements the EMS with speed, consultation and efficiency.

The environmental committee (EC) gathers ideas; works out a plan of action, and keeps the EMS on the school management's agenda.

The EC should also develop new approaches to keep the project interesting and attractive. Everybody connected to the school must have the opportunity to become part of the EC.

Figure 1. Environmental committee -Impucuko Primary school Odendaalsrus Freestate Province.

Step 3 – Initial Environmental Questionnaire

The purpose of this step is to answer the question "What are the main environmental problems in the school? How can we rank them? Where are we now, regarding environmental management at our school, and where do we want to go to?"

To define how to develop a programme that allows to achieve the identified goals and objectives, one should start from an inventory of the existing situation.

This can be done at two levels:

- Environmental management regarding the school management and
- Environmental management in the participating classes.

Issues that can be included in the environmental questionnaire entail:

1) Use of natural resources by the school (quantities of water, energy, raw materials, land).
2) Sources, types and quantities of emissions to the atmosphere.
3) Sources, types and quantities of discharge to water (e.g., into storm water drains, sewers, groundwater and/or rivers).
4) Sources, types and quantities of waste, and details of what happens to it. (Land use and contamination of land)
5) Records of past environmental performance (this should also highlight areas where information on impacts is inadequate).
6) Perceptions of interested parties (e.g., local residents, employees and their representatives, teachers, learners and the general public).
7) Legal requirements.
8) Environmental aspects of products and services (e.g., disposal of the product and its packaging at the end of their useful lives).
9) Incorporation of environmental consideration into design and marketing.
10) Use and disposal of hazardous material.
11) Visual impact, noise, and odours.
12) Opportunities to minimize waste.
13) Knowledge of the environmental impacts of materials and products purchased by the school.
14) Environmental consideration in emergency plans (e.g., the potential for release of toxic chemicals during a fire).

15) Detailed investigation of impacts

The information derived from the environmental questionnaire is the basis for the environmental policy statement or commitment for the whole school.

The purpose of a policy statement is to build a basis to agree on the general direction the school will take with its environmental management system. It should be brief, positive and inspiring. An environmental policy establishes an overall sense of direction and sets the principles of action. It sets the overarching goal on environmental responsibility and performance.

Step 4 - Identify a Theme

The implementation of environmental management should be done in stages.

It should be based on the level of awareness of environmental requirements, aspects (potential environmental impacts), expectations and benefits, and the availability of resources. The result of the environmental questionnaire provides the EC an opportunity to determine which theme the school will address first.

In this project, a choice can be made among four themes:

1) Water (water saving and water pollution)
2) Energy (energy saving and energy sources)
3) Waste (waste prevention and waste treatment)
4) Greening (decorative greening and vegetable gardens)

Other possibilities could be mobility, chemicals, environmentally friendly products, bio-foods etc.

The EC chooses one or two themes and communicates these themes, by means of slogans, posters and letters to the community. The learners should have the opportunity add innovative ideas on the chosen theme.

Step 5 - Develop an Action Plan

After the EC has chosen a theme, an action plan has to be drawn up. At its simplest, an action plan provides the school with a list of things to do and a schedule. The action plan asks in detail:

1) What do we want to achieve (define targets)?
2) What action are we going to take?
3) How action will be taken and when?
4) Who is responsible for implementation?
5) Which schedules allow to implement the actions?
6) What resources do we have?
7) Who is going to be approached outside the school?
8) How are we going to communicate?
9) What actions are we going to take in class?
10) Who will develop the capabilities and support mechanisms necessary to achieve the environmental policy, objectives and targets?

After the plan is drawn up it has to be communicated to the whole school. The EC communicates, informs and consults local authorities, companies and environmental associations about the project.

The senior school management team and the EC identify key people who will be given responsibilities and authority to develop and implement a management programme for the action to be taken.

Objectives should be set at all levels to address the priority issues chosen. These objectives are the overall goals for environmental performance identified in the environmental policy or statement. In setting the objectives the findings from the environmental questionnaire must be taken into account.

Environmental targets can then be set to achieve these objectives within a specified time frame. The targets should be specific and measurable.

Each objective should be broken down into specific targets (measure of performance), that aim to achieve results within the defined time frames.

The school's environmental commitment, policy, objectives and targets should provide a framework for the level of standards to be set. These standards should form part of everyday practice.

An example: photocopying needs rules on the cost-effective use of paper, ink and electricity.

Internal performance criteria, together with external standards, assist the school in developing its own objectives and targets.

In allocating resources the emphasis should be on the prevention of environmental damage. Availability of resources like equipment, controls, process monitoring systems, expertise and management time will determine the success of the implementation of an environmental management system.

The senior school management team should define the responsibilities of relevant personnel in the school management to effectively implement the EMS.

Step 6 - Implement the Action Plan at All Levels

An action plan provides no guarantee that the selected environmental theme or issue will be handled effectively. The distribution of tasks and responsibilities and the use of available management instruments helps to ensure the implementation of the EMS.

There are two groups of environmental management instruments: effect-directed and source-directed instruments.

Effect-directed instruments aim to mitigate or solve effects, e.g., water treatment plants, water saving technology in the toilets, drip irrigation systems to save water, low energy lighting, or noise insulation walls. If correctly applied, these instruments change the quality of the environment without influencing the teachers and learners in changing their behaviour.

Source-directed instruments focus on behavioural changes, e.g., education, information and problem-solving activities.

To be effective, environmental management needs to operate within a structured management system and integrated with the overall management activity of the school.

Environmental management in schools has a key role in building awareness and motivating teachers, learners and employees by explaining the school's environmental values and communicating its commitment to the environmental policy.

Environmental education should not only raise the awareness level of all those who are concerned but also promote a fundamental shift in values and behaviour. This can be done by integrating environmental topics in all learning areas or subjects.

Motivation to continually improve can be enhanced when learners and teachers are recognized for achieving objectives and encouraged to make suggestions that can improve the environmental performance.

Finally, good communication is necessary to establish processes, to report internally and, where desired, externally to the broader community on the environmental activities.

Internal communication is necessary as part of a process that results in environmental awareness, to maintain motivation, to interpret the action plan and to exchange information on progress and on areas that require improvement.

Step 7 - Self Evaluation

A school should review and continually improve its environmental management system.

The following questions can be asked:

1) Have the objectives and targets been reached?
2) If not, were they reasonable and achievable?
3) Did the action plan translate into action?
4) Did learners, teachers and support staff participate in the implementation of the EMS?

After the evaluation the EC must decide how to manage the project in the future, what the new action plan will look like, and how the school can improve its goals. The evaluation must look at the positive and negative aspects as well as the integration of an EMS in the whole school management.

The school will need to develop control mechanisms to ensure that the objectives, targets and standards are met. Whatever control and monitoring mechanisms are put in place, they should be appropriate to the environmental issue dealt with or environmental impact involved. It will also be necessary to make the control and monitoring mechanisms sufficiently explicit so that an environmental review is feasible.

Operational procedures should be defined, documented and updated. The existence of EMS documentation supports awareness of what is required to achieve the schools environmental objectives and enables the evaluation and improvement of the system.

6.2. Themes

Schools have the option to choose one or more areas of environmental action, where they intend to improve their performance:

1. Water

Seventy one percent of the earth's surface is covered by water. 97% is salt water and the planet only hosts 3% of fresh water. Less than 1% of our fresh water is available for agriculture or suitable as drinking water. With the increasing population water is becoming scarce in more and more places worldwide.

The quality of the available water decreases because of pollution. Most diseases in the world are related to water and poor sanitation.

South Africa does not have an abundant supply of water. The average rainfall of 492mm throughout the country is well below the world average of 985mm, this makes South Africa a semi-arid country. Although water is a natural resource, the costs for water treatment, storage and distribution are rising.

(DEAT, http://www.saasta.ac.za/downloads/pdfs/booklet_susdev.pdf, p.12)

Mogono Primary school Phokeng, North West Province.

Figure 2. Push button water taps with basin to catch waste water that is channelled to the vegetable garden.

Within the EMS for primary schools in South Africa, the water-related focus for the school is both, on quantitative (reducing the water use in taps, toilets and gardening) and qualitative aspects (using environmental friendly detergents).

2. Energy

Throughout the world the main sources for energy are fossil fuels such as coal, oil and natural gas. When burnt, these sources cause air pollution and emissions of greenhouse gasses. Fossil fuel resources are limited and deplete, which makes this an unsustainable energy source. There is a need to reduce energy consumption, use fossil energy sources more efficiently and replace fossil fuels by renewable energy sources.

(DEAT, http://www.saasta.ac.za/downloads/pdfs/booklet_susdev.pdf, **p.14)**

Kroonstad, Freestate Province.

Figure 3. Solar water heating facility.

Costs for energy are rising worldwide. Therefore, not only from a sustainable living point of view, but also from an economical point of view, energy is an important issue. The school as an organisation seeks to save energy. All stakeholders should be aware of energy saving methods. The focus is on a reduction in consumption by lighting, heating and electrical appliances.

3. Waste

Population growth and the use of consumer goods result in an ever increasing need for resources. All resources that enter a system result in waste.

There are two ways to deal with waste:

- Waste management, and
- Waste prevention.

Traditional methods of waste management are landfills and incineration. Both methods cause pollution and nuisance.

Prevention of pollution is a low-cost waste approach that views solid and hazardous waste as potential resources that can be recycled, reused or not been produced in the first place.

Kopanang Primary school,Magogong, North West Province.

Figure 4. Learners clean-up project.

The school as an organisation and all stakeholders produce waste during their everyday actions. The whole school seeks to reduce its amount of waste by improving the stakeholders 's attitude towards waste production and waste treatment.

The focus is on waste prevention (double sided copies, using reusable glass containers and lunch boxes) and sorting of waste (in appropriate waste bins, composting organic waste and arranging proper disposal of hazardous material).

4. Greening

School gardens should be dealt with at two levels:

- Decorative gardens, and
- Food gardens

Both levels have a substantial, educational and environmental value. Gardens provide materials to be used in lessons, they can provide food, they can be used for environment related activities and organic waste can be used as compost.

Whereas the themes of energy, water and waste deal with environmental problems, greening is about a positive contribution to the environment.

Hlaboloha Primary school Bothaville, Freestate Province.

Figure 5. Vegetable gardens maintained with community participation.

The focus is on qualitative aspects (decorative gardens and vegetable gardens to support the school's feeding scheme) and environmentally friendly gardening techniques (efficient use of water, mulching and using composted organic waste as fertilizer). Also collateral effects are involved, as sometimes products from the vegetable garden are used by the kitchen of the school or sold to the local community.

6.3. Supporting Methods and Material

The following materials are supplied to assist the schools in implementing an EMS:

6.3.1. Guidelinebook

Raath et al., 2009.

Figure 6. Cover of the Guidelinebook, for schools in South Africa.

A guideline book: "Education for sustainable living" (244 pp., assessable on the website: http://www.vub.ac.be/MEKO/projects/ safrica/Project 2009.htm) provides practical guidelines for schools to establish and to implement an EMS (Figure 6).

The book contains an introduction to EMS for basic schools as a stepwise process and an explanation about how EMS articulate with the terms of reference in the National Curriculum Statement (NCS) for the 2 highest years of primary schools in South Africa.

It also contains practical experiments for environmental learning for the themes: water, waste, energy and greening.

6.3.2. Toolkit with Experiments

A "toolbox" is supplied, containing 12 experiments that illustrate the themes water, waste, energy and greening. These experiments aim at making the explanation of the four environmental areas in the guideline book more tangible.

The use of the "toolbox" was demonstrated to the teachers by means of hands-on activity training.

Figure 7. The toolbox (examples: water catcher and solar stove).

6.3.3. Training and Info-Sessions

During the info-sessions, educational and management professionals from Universities and from the Flemish Government, explain the necessary steps and practical aspects of the implementation of EMS in schools.

The training addresses the environmental policies, objectives and targets. Examples are provided on how to conduct an energy review, or how to draw up rules to use resources in an environmentally responsible and cost effective way.

The environmental trainers and representatives of the other stakeholders from each school are instructed during these info-sessions to become familiar with the environmental experiments in the toolbox.

The outcome of these workshops has been published on: http://www.vub.ac.be/MEKO/projects/safrica/Project2009.htm

Figure 8. Construction of a solar stove.

6.3.4. Awards

The awards for schools that perform well are an essential component of any EMS. Besides the internal awards system developed in the framework of the Flemish project, the project is linked with the international Eco-school "Green Flag" system, that is in SA operated by the Wildlife and Environmental Society of South Africa (WESSA, http://www.wessa.org.za/index.php/Programs/Eco-Schools.html). Both systems contribute to the wider visibility of the projects.

To grant the awards, a checklist was used to evaluate the implementation of the EMS and environmental learning. The application of the checklist and allocation of awards is done by an independent official from the "Environmental Care at Schools" (Milieuzorg op school/MOS) project from Flanders (Flemish Government, 2007 and 2008). Four levels of awards can be reached:

- Level 1: Participation in the system, the school sets its environment education targets, develops a vision of environmental performance and cross-curricular activities.
- Level 2: Completion of a performance portfolio for one EMS cycle (any subject: water, waste, energy or greening)
- Level 3: Completion of a performance portfolio for two EMS cycles (two subjects) AND there are indications of progress in the environmental performance of the school.
- Level 4: Full application of the system (four)themes) AND detailed monitoring data AND evidence of progress.

Figure 9. Award for environmental performances.

Chapter 7

Evaluation of the EMS

7.1. Monitoring

After 6 years, the schools and their teachers are still highly motivated. The project offers an answer to real, unmet and urgent needs. But it seems to be more difficult to start the EMS.

To evaluate the efficiency of the project and the general objectives of the EMS implementation in primary schools, quantified results are required. Gathering and dealing with these data is a core objective of the project.

Monitoring of an EMS in primary schools entails 4 aspects:

1) Monitoring the physical environmental aspects. This is related to questions such as "how many litres of water did we save?", "How many litres of water did we save?", "How much electricity did we save?", etc. This part of the monitoring addresses environmental gains and benefits of the project.
2) Managerial aspects of the implementation of the EMS relate mainly to four areas: school policy (e.g. the environmental declaration as a part of the school policy), organization of the process, implementation of activities and integration of the EMS in the curriculum.
3) Pedagogical aspects relate to questions such as "does the EMS (sufficiently) contribute to the National Curriculum Statement as established by the education authorities?"; "to which extent does it contribute to the educational targets of the school?".

4) Collateral effects are consequences of the use of an EMS that are not primarily intended by the instruments, but that are nevertheless real and important. Among others they include:
    - o - Acceptance of ownership of the school by the learners,
    - o - Cost-consciousness on environmental resources and assets, such as energy, water, waste and gardening products (vegetables, flowers),
    - o - Sociability, which entails responsibility, dealing with the challenges of nowadays society and sustainable solutions,
    - o - (mental) health and wellbeing: less vandalism, focus on cooperation, consultation and participation.

Measurement proved to be difficult, since not all schools work according to the guidelines for the different environmental themes and the managerial aspects of the EMS.

Therefore, in 2006-2008, a detailed questionnaire (in addition to the checklist for the awards) was set up to gather data on managerial and environmental aspects. This approach allowed wide coverage at minimum expenses. The questionnaire allows to measure what teachers know (knowledge and information), what they like and dislike (values and preferences), and what they think (attitudes and beliefs) as well as to inventory and evaluate the experiences that have taken place.

The questionnaires were completed by 39 schools during 3 surveys:

1) Survey: prior to the start of the EMS (immediately following the Training of Trainers (ToT)-workshop in 2006),
2) Survey: by the end of the first year (first management cycle) of the EMS in 2007, and
3) Survey: by the end of the project (second management cycle), followed by a final ground truth check in 2008.

The results were introduced in a GIS database and treated statistically to detect and analyse correlations between different aspects of the EMS.

The questionnaire survey for the schools addressed four aspects of the use of EMS:

1) Integration of the environment in the **management** of the school (Managerial aspects),

2) **Emphasis** on the environment in the curriculum (Pedagogical aspects),
3) **Attitudes** of teachers and learners towards the environment - Educational benefit (Collateral aspects),
4) Performances on 4 **environmental issues**:
   a) Water,
   b) Waste,
   c) Energy,
   d) Greening.

The performance of the schools according to each of these aspects is measured using identical "scaling checklists" (Smith, 1993, p.18). These checklists entail 72 questions. Each question is related to one of the 4 aspects mentioned above, with 6 to 16 questions per aspect. The underlying idea is to measure the performance of each school for each aspect in a representative, comparable and objective way, taking relevant variables into account.

A completed checklist is rated by allocating scores for the answers. The scores per answer range from 0-4:

4: Yes
3: Yes, in some way
2: No, in some way
1: No, not at all
0: Not applicable

Each question has been formulated in a way that the option 'yes' indicates a positive engagement, while 'no, not at all' indicates a negative engagement. No weights have been allocated to the different questions, each question is regarded as equally important for the aspect to which the question refers.

The following questions have been answered by the participating schools during the surveys (T0-T2):

7.1.1. Management

The questions in table 1 address the managerial organisation of the EMS in the schools: Questions such as 'the school has a structured step-by-step-plan' or 'the school has an environmental task-group', are used as indicators for the planning of environmental actions. The task group leads and coordinates the implementation and the maintenance of the environmental management system. 'The Environmental Management System is communicated to the stakeholders' to keep all members of the school community informed about the implementation of environmental care at school. After this, the environmental task group can start with establishing the inventory, using the questions listed in tables 1 to 7 as a check-list. In "this way, the results of the stock-taking of the environmental situation can be seen through a visual presentation (diagrams, graphs etc.)" (Van Volsem et al., 1997, p.51) and bottlenecks of the projects can be detected.

Table 1. Questions related to managerial aspects of implementing an EMS at schools

1) Environmental management is part of the vision of our school
2) The governing body, teachers, learners and administration staff had the opportunity to contribute to our school's environmental policy
3) The Environmental Management System is communicated to the stakeholders
4) The school sets proper objectives to control the quality of its environmental projects
5) The school integrates environmental concerns into the schools regulations
6) Top management supports environmental projects at the school
7) The school has an environmental task group
8) The objectives and responsibilities of the environmental task group are clearly described
9) The organisation of the school includes and promotes environmental activities
10) There is a way in which stakeholders can make suggestions to improve environmental performance of the school
11) Teachers are prepared to invest time in the implementation of environmental projects
12) The school has a structured step-by-step plan to implement an environmental management system
13) The task group assesses the implementation of EMS
14) The task group assesses the results of EMS
15) The school organises environmental activities
16) The environmental consequences of all decisions and actions are taken into account by the school

7.1.2. Emphasis

Table 2. Questions related to pedagogical aspects of implementing EMS at schools

1. All teachers integrate the environment in their learning areas
2. Teachers work together to integrate the environment in learning programs
3. Environmental learning activities should be integrated in each of the 8 learning areas. Indicate in how many learning areas this applies. (1 = one or two, 2 = three or four, 3=five or six, 4 = seven or eight)
4. Our top management supports the integration of the environment in the curriculum
5. Environmental training influenced the environmental management of the school
6. In the school the environment is regarded as the common responsibility of all teachers
7. The problem of water pollution is integrated in learning areas
8. The problem of waste is integrated in learning areas
9. The efficient use of energy is integrated in learning areas
10. The benefit of gardens is integrated in learning areas
11. The teachers use the school grounds for their lessons
12. The teachers use the surrounding neighbourhood as an outdoor classroom
13. There are environmental books and magazines available to the learners at the school

The questions listed in table 2 aim at monitoring the integration of environmental concepts and issues in the learning outcomes of the different learning areas, as foreseen in the National Curriculum Statement of the South African Department for Education (http://www.mml.co.za/docs/The%20Revised%20National%20Curriculum%20Statement.pdf).

7.1.3. Attitude

Table 3. Questions concerning collateral aspects related to implementing an EMS at schools

1. The teachers are responsible users of resources
2. The learners are responsible users of resources
3. Littering is not a problem at the school
4. The teachers are proud of their school
5. The teachers feel responsible for their school
6. The learners are proud of their school
7. The learners feel responsible for their school
8. The school regards environment, safety and health as integrated issues
9. The school regards environmental management as the most cost-effective way to manage the school
10. Environmental education is the best way to prepare learners for citizenship
11. Learners are critical thinkers and focused on problem solving
12. Learners regard the school as a place of living and not only for learning
13. Hundred percent of the school time is spent on educational activities
14. The community regards the school as an essential educational facility.

The questions in table 3 refer to collateral aspects of the EMS: is environmental care internalized in the attitude of the stakeholders of the school? Do teachers and learners feel responsible for the school's impact of the environment? Does the implementation of the EMS have an impact on the behaviour of teachers and learners? How do teachers, learners and the community perceive the school?

7.1.4. Performance on 4 Environmental Issues

"A thorough inventory of the environmental situation at the school, provides a better view of the use of water and energy in the school as well as an insight into (...) the green spaces (or lack of them) both within and around the school (and) the origin of waste." (Van Volsem et al., 1997, p.48) Therefore, the inventory contains 4 checklists, aiming at evaluating the environmental aspects 'water', 'waste', 'energy' and 'greening':

7.1.4.1. Water

Table 4. Questions related to environmental performance on water quantity and quality

1. Water taps are regularly controlled for leaks and repaired
2. Toilets are regularly controlled for leaks and repaired
3. Toilets are equipped with water saving technologies or devices
4. Rainwater is harvested for reuse
5. Environmental friendly detergents products are used by the school
6. Water wise gardening techniques are used to use water effectively
7. Water meter is read regularly to managed water use
8. Maintenance staff are aware of the importance to save water

Table 4 lists the questions on water use.

7.1.4.2. Waste

Table 5. Questions related to environmental performance on waste

1. The school sorts all the solid waste generated by the school in appropriate bins.
2. There are enough appropriate waste bins on the school grounds
3. There are enough appropriate waste bins in all the classrooms
4. All organic waste produced by the school is composted in the school premises
5. Copies of documents and computer prints are always made on both sides of paper
6. The staff sets an example in the prevention of waste generation
7. The school provides an example to the learners by purchasing environmental friendly products
8. Minimising of waste is promoted (E.g. by using reusable glass containers, lunch boxes etc.)
9. Sufficient arrangements are made for the proper disposal of hazardous material (E.g. batteries, acid, etc.)

Table 5 shows how performance of waste is addressed.

7.1.4.3. Energy

Table 6. Questions related to environmental performance on "Energy"

1. The school uses low energy lighting systems
2. Solar power is used wherever appropriate
3. The school buildings are well isolated to reduce energy use for cooling and warming
4. The geyser systems of the school are isolated with geyser blankets and the temperature setting is not higher than 600 C
5. Some equipment work on rechargeable batteries to save energy (school gate, school bell, intercom system etc.)
6. The whole school population is made aware of small energy saving measures (like switching off equipment not in use)

Table 6 lists the questions related to energy use.

7.1.4.4. Greening

Table 7. Questions related to environmental performance on energy

1. The school has an indigenous decorative garden.
2. Efficient use of water form part of the planning of the school gardens
3. Compost produced by the school is used to fertilize the gardens
4. Mulching is used in the gardens to conserve water
5. A vegetable garden supports the feeding scheme of the school
6. Products produced in the vegetable garden are sold to the community

Table 7 provides the questions used to monitor the performance of the schools on greening their local environment.

For the quantification and comparison of the managerial aspects, average results of the scores of all parameters for the aspects "management", "emphasis", "attitude" and "environmental aspects (water, waste, energy and greening)" have been calculated per type of school. The average survey-results have been re-allocated to scores, ranging from 1-4 (analogously to the scores, allocated to the original list of questions):

- Score 1: average score ≥ 1.0 and <1.5 (the answer to most questions was ("no" or "not at all")
- Score 2: average score ≥ 1.5 and <2.5
- Score 3: average score ≥ 2.5 and <3.5
- Score 4: average score ≥ 3.5 and ≤ 4.0 (the answer to most questions was ("yes")

Further on, this chapter refers to scores 1-2 as 'low' scores, while scores 3-4 are 'high' scores, independent from the variation of the scores between different parameters, related to the same aspect.

7.2. RESULTS

The monitoring results in the schools revealed significant and positive effects of the projects:

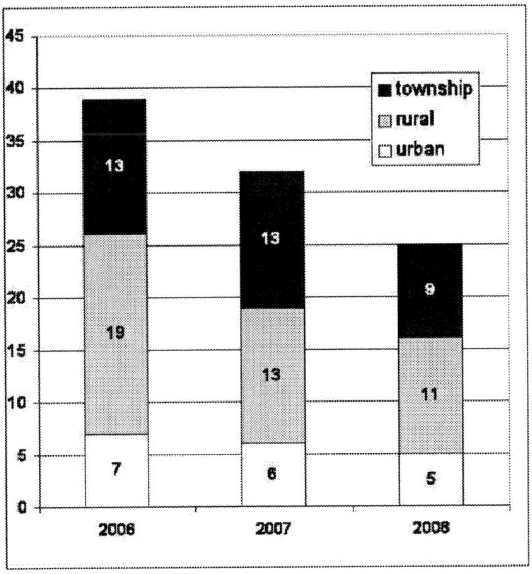

Luc Hens et al., 2010 (b).

Figure 10. Number of schools in the survey, 2006-2008, per type of school.

7.2.1. Surveys and Profiles of Schools

As shown in figure 10, 3 surveys were carried out using the questionnaires: A baseline survey (T0) in 2006 (38schools), a survey following up the first management cycle (T1) in 2007 (32 schools) and a final survey following the second management cycle (T2) in 2008 (25 schools).

The results were verified by a follow-up survey, performed 1 month after the final survey in 25 schools.

Profile of the Schools

Each school provided data about enrolment, area of residence, mode of learner's transportation and number of electrical appliances, such as computers. These data allow classifying the participating schools into 3 categories:

7 Urban schools are located in cities or villages. They are medium-sized (560 learners average) and the classes are relatively small (25 learners per teacher in average). The main mode of transport of the learners is by car. The average number of learners per computer is 0.02.

19 Rural schools are located near (remote) farms and in rural areas. The participating rural schools are small (350 learners on average) and the classes

are relatively big (32 learners per teacher in average). The main mode of transport is by public busses. The average number of computers per learner is 0.02, but 50% of the rural schools don't have computers at all.

13 Township schools are located in former settlements of the apartheid regime. The participating township schools are large (1003 learners average) with relatively big classes (32 learners per teacher in average). Most of the learners walk to school. The average number of computers per learner is 0.01 (half as many as in urban schools), and every participating township school has at least 1 computer.

The number of monitored schools declined from 39 schools at the baseline-survey (T0) to 32 schools at T1 and 25 schools at T2. Two schools were closed during the study period and in the 2nd survey, not all schools have been visited by the researchers, due to a lack of time and manpower to cover the huge distances between the participating schools.

7.2.2. Management

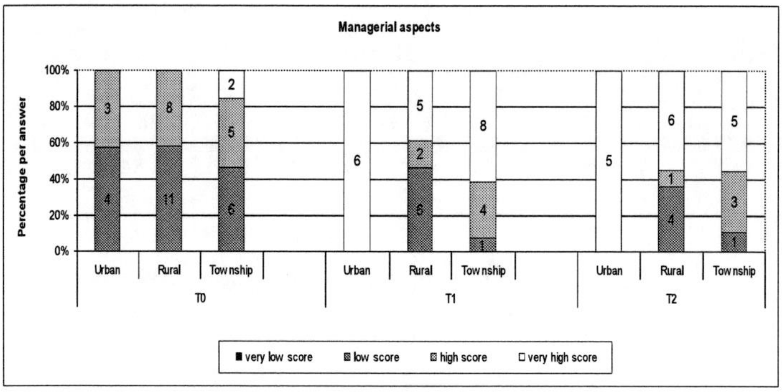

Luc Hens et al., 2010 (a).

Figure 11. Number of schools, by scores for management, by survey and by type of school.

The integration of the environment in the management of the school was measured by addressing different managerial aspects, such as "Environmental management is part of the vision of our school", "The school integrates environmental concerns into school regulations", etc.

Before the schools started the implementation of the EMS (baseline survey, T0), 40% of the urban schools (3 out of 7 schools), 40% of the rural schools (8 out of 19 schools) and 50% of the township schools (7 out of 13 schools) used one or another form of environmental management. At the 2nd survey, 100% of the urban schools, 60% of the rural schools and 90% of the township schools achieved high scores for the managerial aspects of the EMS.

Thus, in particular urban and township schools successfully implemented an EMS into the school management during the study.

During the 1st survey (T1), 6 rural schools and 1 township school had low scores for management. The reasons for this differ from school to school. One remarkable feature is that in none of these 7 schools the task group assessed the implementation and the results of the EMS. Five of the 6 rural schools with low scores in T1 did not develop a step-by-step plan.

7.2.3.Emphasis

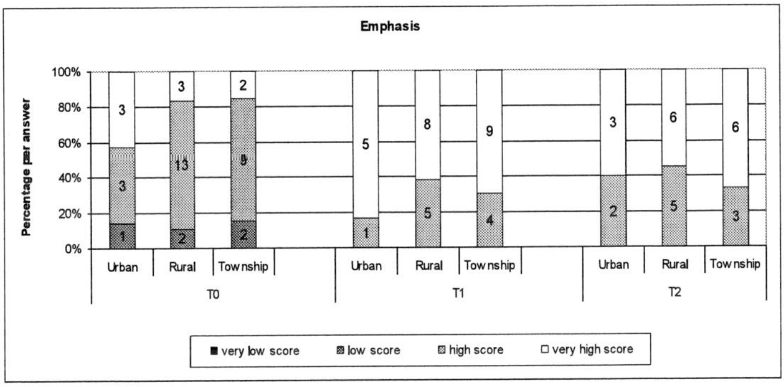

Luc Hens et al., 2010 (a).

Figure 12. Number of schools, by scores for emphasis, by survey and by type of school.

Emphasis on the environment in the curriculum was measured addressing different aspects, such as “Teachers integrate the environment in their learning areas”, “In our school the environment is regarded as the common responsibility of all teachers” etc.

At the start of the study (baseline survey, T0), 85% of all participating schools emphasize the environment in the curriculum: 6 out of 7 urban schools, 16 out of 20 rural schools and 11 out of 13 township schools reached high or very high scores. By the end of the project, this figure increased to 100%: none of the participating schools had low scores. 60% of all schools (3 urban schools, 6 rural school and 6 township schools) had very high scores.

The common reason for 10 schools showing high, but not very high, scores in the 2nd survey (2 urban schools, 5 rural schools and 3 township schools) is that these schools either had no environmental books and magazines available for the learners, or the benefit of the gardens was not integrated in the learning areas.

7.2.4. Attitude

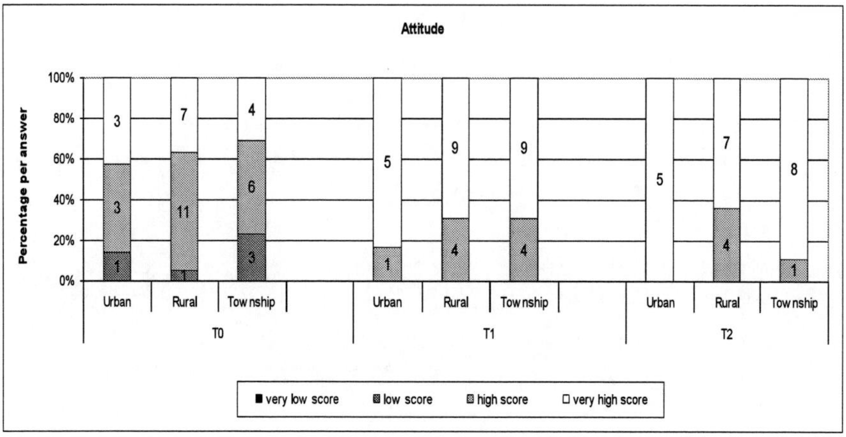

Luc Hens et al., 2010 (a).

Figure 13. Number of schools, by scores for attitude, by survey and by type of school.

Different aspects (such as "Teachers and learners are responsible users of resources", "Teachers and learners feel responsible for their school", etc.) allow to measure the attitudes of teachers and learners towards the environment (the educational benefit). At the moment of the baseline survey (T0), 85% of the urban schools, 95% of the rural schools and 75% of the township schools indicated an outspoken attention for attitude related parameters. By the end of the project, all participating schools had high or very high scores for attitude. The schools with 'high scores' for attitude had low scores for the parameters ''The school regards environmental management as the most cost effective way to manage the school'', ''Learners are critical thinkers and focus on problem solving'' and/or ''The community regards the school as an essential educational facility''.

7.2.5. Performance on 4 Environmental Issues

7.2.5.1. Water

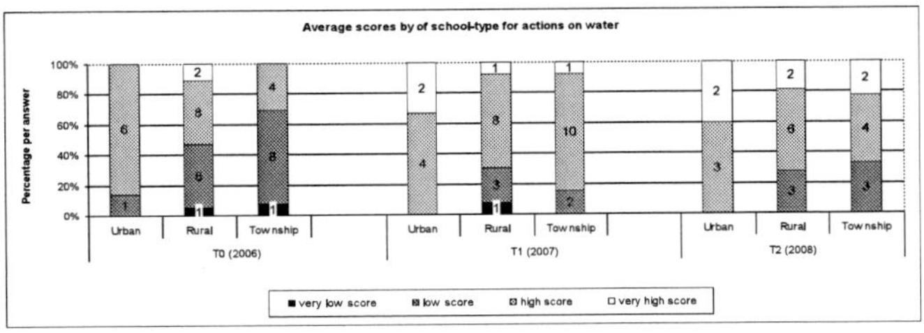

Luc Hens et al., 2010 (b).

Figure 14. Number of schools, by scores for actions on water, by survey and by type of school.

At the beginning of the monitoring period (T0), 90% of the urban schools, but only 30% of the township schools and 55% of the rural schools acted to save water (scores higher than 2.4). Two years later (T2), 100% of the urban schools and 70% of the rural and township schools implemented actions on water.

The least popular water related actions were "Toilets are equipped with water saving technologies or devices" and "Rainwater is harvested for reuse".

The most popular activities were "Water taps and toilets are regularly controlled for leaks and repaired".

The less popular water related actions are cost-intensive (water saving technologies and installations for the collection of rainwater cost money), while the favourite actions are cost free (controlling for and repairing leaks is a task, which can be carried out by the school's maintenance staff).

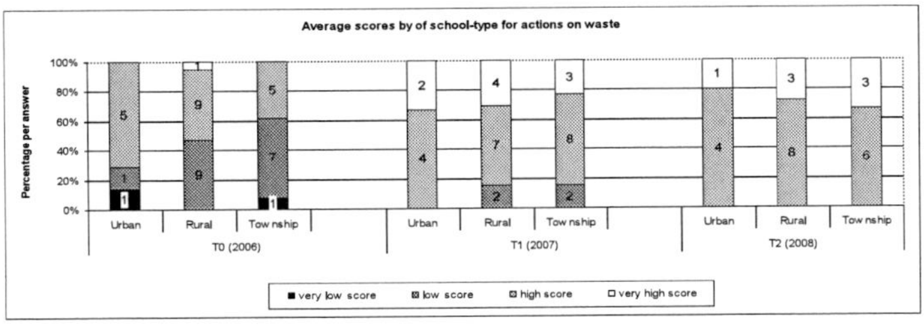

Luc Hens et al., 2010 (b).

Figure 15. Number of schools, by scores for actions on waste, by survey and by type of school.

During the baseline survey, 70% of the urban schools, but only 50% of the rural schools and 40% of the township schools cared about the waste the school produces. After two years (T2), all schools have positive waste-related scores (score 3, light grey) and 30% of the schools even have high waste-related scores (white: score 4, corresponding with average values between 3.5 and 4).

The least popular waste related action was "Sufficient arrangements are made for the proper disposal of hazardous material (E.g. batteries, acid, etc.)".

The most popular activities were "Copies of documents and computer prints are always made on both sides of paper" and "There are enough appropriate waste bins in all the classrooms".

Again, as for water related actions, cost-free or low-cost actions were the favourite actions.

In South Africa, especially in rural areas, waste collection is a problem, because the distances between waste recycling enterprises and schools are too large. Waste recycling companies regard it as economically inefficient to collect paper, glass or plastic from remote schools. Therefore, arrangements for proper disposal waste are rarely made in township or rural schools.

7.2.5.2. Energy

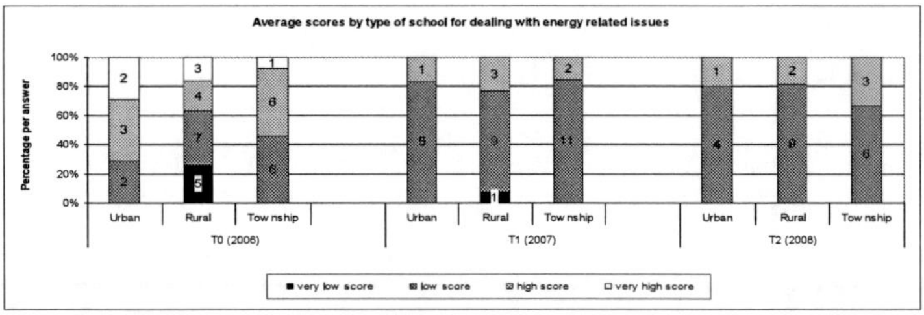

Luc Hens et al., 2010 (b).

Figure 16. Number of schools, by scores for actions on energy, by survey and by type of school.

At the baseline survey, 70% of the urban schools, 40% of the rural schools and 50% of the township schools had high energy-related scores. In the 2nd survey, these figures drop to 20% for all types of schools.

The energy-related activities did not improve during the monitoring period, on the contrary; for all school types there is a decline between the baseline and the 1st survey.

A methodological reason might be at the basis of this result:

Figure 16 only represents average scores, calculated from the answers to 6 energy-related questions. During the baseline survey, over 50% of the schools indicated ''not applicable'' as an answer to the energy-related questions "does the school use solar power?" and "does the school use rechargeable batteries?". At the occasions of the 1st and 2nd survey, most schools answered ''no'' to these questions. Therefore, the score changes from ''0'' (not applicable) to ''1'' (no, not at all), resulting in a relatively low average value for energy-related actions, as ''0'' values are not included in the calculation of average scores.

At the time of the baseline survey, 35% of all schools indicated that their buildings are well-insulated (scores >3). In the 1st survey, this figure drops to 12%. Probably, the schools reviewed their definitions of 'well isolated' and made a more realistic assessment of their insulation efforts. The ground truth check revealed that no single building at any of the schools was well isolated, according to international standards.

The ground truth check equally showed that more than half of the schools did not use the stand-by or energy saving modes for their electrical appliances and the thermostat of their fridges were put on the coldest setting, which might be an indicator for a lack of awareness on energy saving opportunities.

7.2.5.3. Greening

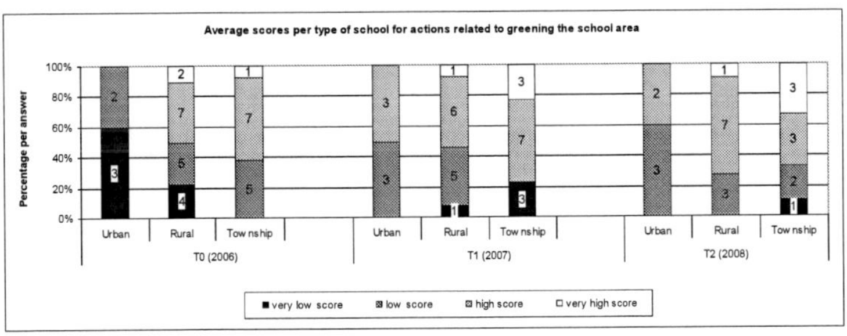

Luc Hens et al., 2010 (b).

Figure 17. Number of schools, per score for actions on greening, per survey and per type of school.

At the baseline survey, none of the urban schools, 50% of the rural schools and 60% of the township schools had high greening related scores. At the 1st survey, 50% of the urban schools, 50% of the rural schools and 75% of the township schools show high greening-related scores. Thus, at least at 3 urban schools and at 4 township schools the greening situation improved after the introduction of an EMS.

7.2.6. Correlations between the 7 Aspects of the EMS

Each school takes action on water, waste, energy and greening. As discussed above, these four issues were measured in analogy with the managerial, emphasis and attitude aspects.

The correlations between the average scores for the different aspects of the EMS in rural and in township schools are shown in table 8. No correlations have been detected in urban schools.

Table 8. Pearson correlation coefficients between the average scores of all aspects of the EMS in the 1st survey in rural and township schools

	Water	Waste	Energy	Greening
Manage	.623**	.425*	.197	.510**
Emphasis	.683**	.450**	.333	.582**
Attitude	.713**	.395*	.248	.483**

*Correlation is significant at the 0.05 level (2-tailed); **correlation is significant at the 0.01 level (2-tailed).

In the baseline-survey, schools with high levels of communication and participation also performed well on the themes water and energy.

In the 1st survey the strongest correlations were found between managerial aspects and environmental activities related to water and greening (as shown in table 8). In the 2nd survey, only greening was strongly correlated with managerial aspects.

Rural schools show the highest values for correlations between managerial aspects and environmental activities related to water and waste during the 1st survey.

In the 2nd survey, also greening was strongly correlated with management. This is because most rural schools first opted for water and waste as main environmental themes and only later greening was found to be a theme for environmental action. The statement "Teachers invest time in the implementation of the EMS" is strongly correlated with "greening".

Especially activity-related managerial aspects (promotion and organization of activities) are correlated with the environmental activities in the 1st survey.

Table 8 does not reveal different patterns of behaviour for rural and township schools: In township schools, activities have to be stimulated to achieve high scores for environmental management.

Greening seems to be very sensitive for managerial aspects. Greening requires indeed more planning, organization and co-ordination than other environmental themes. Since the number of cases in this study is limited (9 township schools, 13 rural schools and 3 urban schools in the 2nd survey), the statistical results may not be significant. In the future, more research is necessary, based on larger cohorts of schools, to allow for reliable calculations and conclusions.

In township schools, garden related activities are strongly correlated with the scores for management, emphasis and attitude. Water and waste are correlated with emphasis scores.

For the urban schools, no correlations are calculated, due to the low number of urban schools (5) in the 1st survey.

Chapter 8

CONCLUSION

An environmental management system (an EMS) provides opportunities to involve learners in the management of the school and to integrate the environment into the school curriculum, and it contributes to ownership of all those involved in the process.

It provides schools with a structure to address environmental concerns through the allocation of resources, assignment of responsibilities, and ongoing evaluation of practices, procedures and processes within the school.

In general, all participating schools integrate environment into the management of the school. Independent from the type of school (urban, rural or township), 80% of the monitored schools did integrate environment into the management of the school, while at the beginning of the project only 45% of the schools applied one or another form of environmental management.

In comparison with the results of other environmental projects in South Africa, the overall results are similar in schools that committed themselves to efforts related to environmental care. For example, comparing the results in this chapter with the "Adopt–a Schoolyard" competition in 2001 and 2002, where in 43 schools in Mpumalanga (a province east of Gauteng and the Limpopo Province), the integration of environmental issues into the curriculum rose from 51% in 2001 to 74% in 2002 (De Lange, 2004, p.139). These are nearly the same results as presented and discussed in this chapter: At the baseline-survey, 51% (20/39) of all schools performed well on water- and waste-related environmental actions, while at the second survey 76% (19/25) of all schools performed well on water-related environmental actions, and 100% performed well on waste-related environmental actions.

Integration of the environment into the management of the school is correlated with the environmental performance of the schools, except for energy (Hens et al., 2010 (a)).

Both managerial aspects and environmental care are well elaborated at the same moment. On the other hand, these correlations might indicate that a well elaborated organisational implementation of the EMS is a necessity if a school wants to perform well on environmental care.

Assessment of the integration of an EMS, a step-by-step-plan, environmental activities and educational resources are the most important organizational aspects with impact on the environmental performance of all schools in the project; however, there are significant differences between the different types of schools (rural, urban, township). Because the number of schools in this sample is limited, no reliable statistical evidence is offered to prove this hypothesis. Further research with more participating schools is necessary to fully understand these differences (Hens et al. 2010 (b)).

The strategies, instruments and tools developed during this project are applicable to any school, worldwide. Possibilities for objective and comparable measurement of the managerial aspects of EMS have been achieved.

ACKNOWLEDGMENTS

The project is organised as a co-operation among the Faculty of Education Sciences of the North-West University (Potchefstroom Campus), Museum Park (Pretoria) and the Human Ecology Department of the Vrije Universiteit Brussel. The project is equally supported by the provincial departments of education of the involved provinces and the "MOS – Milieuzorg op school" (environmental care at schools) group of the LNE department of the Flemish Community of Belgium.

---

[1] Environment, Nature and Energy

REFERENCES

LITERATURE

[1] De Lange, A.M. (2004). An Evaluation of the implementation of the "School Environmental Policy and Management Plan" in schools in Mpumalanga. University of South Africa (Unpublished PhD-Thesis).

[2] Flemish Government (2008) Annual Report MOS (Environmental Care in schools) November 2007–October 2008. Department for Environment, Nature and Energy (LNE), Brussels.

[3] Hens, L., Nath, B. (2003) *The Johannesburg Conference. Environment, Development and Sustainability*. Springer, Dordrecht.

[4] Hens, L., Wiedemann, T., Raath, S., Stone, R., Renders, P., Craenhals, E., Richter, B. (2010 (a)) "Monitoring environmental management at primary schools in South Africa", *Journal of Cleaner Production*, 18, 666–677.

[5] Hens, L., Wiedemann, T., Raath, S., Stone, R., Renders, P., Craenhals, E. (2010 (b)) "Performance of newly implemented Environmental Management Systems in primary schools in South Africa", *Journal of Environmental Management*, 91, 906–917.

[6] Raath, S., Stone, R., Van Heerden, M. (2009) Education for sustainable living. North-West University, Museum Park and VUB, Brussels and Pretoria.

[7] Van Volsem, S., Vens, V. (Eds.) (1997) Schools, Universities and the Environment.

[8] International Seminar on Environmental Care and EMS in Schools and Universities. VUB, Department of Human Ecology, Brussels.

WEBSITES

[9] Department of Environmental Affairs and Tourism (DEAT), South Africa, An Easy Guide to Sustainable Development: http://www.saasta.ac.za/downloads/pdfs/booklet_susdev.pdf (accessed 12.05.2010)
[10] Flemish Government, Department for Environment, Nature and Energy (LNE): Environmental Care in Schools in Flanders Region (MOS): http://www.lne.be/doelgroepen/onderwijs/mos (accessed 12.05.2010).
[11] Human Ecology Department: http://www.humanecology.be (accessed 12.05.2010).
[12] Information about the project ''Building Capacity for Sustainable living - Implementation of Environmental Management in Primary Schools in South Africa'': http://www.vub.ac.be/MEKO/projects/safrica/ southafr.html (accessed 12.05.2010)
[13] ''Sustainable Living in Schools: Newsletter 2'', July/October 2006: http://www.vub.ac.be/MEKO/projects/safrica/newslet2.doc (accessed 12.05.2010).
[14] A guideline book: "Education for sustainable living": http://www.vub.ac.be/MEKO/projects/safrica/Project2009.htm (accessed 12.05.2010)
[15] South African Revised National Curriculum Statement: http://www.mml.co.za/docs/The%20Revised%20National%20Curriculum%20Statement.pdf (accessed 12.05.2010);
[16] Wildlife and Environment Society of South Africa (WESSA), Eco-schools Programme: http://www.wessa.org.za/index.php/Programs/Eco-Schools.html (accessed 12.05.2010).

INDEX

A

acid, 33, 41
advantages, viii
Africa, 3, 19
agriculture, 19
allocating, 16, 29
assessment, 42
assets, 28
authorities, 27

B

batteries, 33, 34, 41, 42
Belgium, 3, 49
buildings, 34, 42

C

citizenship, 10, 32
class, 16
classroom, 31
coal, 20
collateral, 23, 32
community, 7, 9, 11, 12, 15, 17, 22, 32, 34, 39
competition, 47
compost, 22
composting, 22
consciousness, 28
conservation, 6
consumer goods, 21
consumption, 1, 21
contamination, 14
cooling, 34
correlation, vii, 44
correlation coefficient, 44
correlations, 28, 43, 44, 45, 48
cost, 16, 21, 25, 32, 39, 40, 41
curricula, viii
curriculum, vii, 3, 7, 8, 11, 12, 27, 29, 31, 38, 47
cycles, 26

D

database, 28
demonstrations, 10
detergents, 20, 33
drinking water, 19

E

electricity, 1, 7, 16, 27
endangered species, 10
energy consumption, 20
environmental awareness, 17
environmental impact, vii, 2, 14, 15, 18
environmental issues, viii, 1, 29, 47

environmental policy, 15, 16, 17, 30
environmental resources, 8, 28
equipment, 16, 34
experiences, 1, 28
expertise, 16

F

farms, 36

G

groundwater, 14
guidelines, vii, 11, 24, 28

H

hypothesis, 48

I

impacts, 12, 14, 15
insulation, 17, 42
integration, vii, 18, 27, 31, 37, 47, 48
international standards, 42

L

landfills, 21
leaks, 33, 40
learners, vii, 1, 10, 12, 14, 15, 17, 18, 28, 29, 30, 31, 32, 33, 36, 38, 39, 47
learning, 1, 2, 3, 9, 10, 11, 12, 17, 24, 26, 31, 32, 38
learning outcomes, 31
legislation, 12
Limpopo, 3, 47
local authorities, 16
local community, 23

M

magazines, 31, 38
majority, 10
management, vii, 1, 2, 3, 7, 8, 9, 10, 11, 13, 14, 15, 16, 17, 18, 21, 25, 28, 30, 31, 32, 34, 36, 37, 39, 44, 45, 47, 48, 51
manpower, 36
marketing, 12, 14
meter, 33
monitoring, vii, 2, 3, 16, 18, 26, 27, 31, 35, 40, 42
motivation, 17

N

natural gas, 20
natural resources, 14
natural sciences, 9
NCS, 24
networking, 13
noise, 14, 17
nuisance, 21

O

oil, 20
opportunities, viii, 1, 14, 43, 47
ownership, 28, 47

P

packaging, 14
performance, vii, 1, 14, 15, 16, 17, 18, 26, 29, 30, 33, 34, 48
physical environment, 27
plants, 17
pollution, 1, 8, 15, 19, 20, 21, 31
population growth, 1
portfolio, 26
positive attitudes, 12
Potchefstroom, 49
prevention, 6, 12, 15, 16, 21, 22, 33

primary school, vii, 2, 3, 9, 20, 24, 27, 51
problem solving, 10, 32, 39
problem-solving, 17
project, vii, 2, 3, 6, 7, 10, 12, 13, 15, 16, 18, 21, 26, 27, 28, 38, 39, 47, 48, 49, 52

Q

questioning, 11

R

rainfall, 19
raw materials, 14
recommendations, iv
recycling, 10, 41
relevance, 7
renewable energy, 20
resources, 1, 2, 6, 8, 15, 16, 20, 21, 25, 32, 39, 47, 48
rural areas, 36, 41

S

scaling, 29
school community, 9, 12, 30
settlements, 36
social sciences, 9
solid waste, 33
South Africa, i, iii, vii, 2, 3, 7, 11, 19, 20, 23, 24, 26, 31, 41, 47, 51, 52
stakeholders, 8, 13, 21, 22, 25, 30, 32
storage, 19
support staff, 18
survey, vii, 28, 34, 35, 36, 37, 38, 39, 40, 41, 42, 43, 44, 45, 47
sustainability, 10
sustainable development, 3, 7

T

temperature, 34
time frame, 16
training, 3, 24, 25, 31
transport, 36
transportation, 36

V

vandalism, 28
vegetables, 28
vision, 2, 6, 26, 30, 37

W

waste, vii, 1, 7, 9, 14, 15, 19, 21, 22, 23, 24, 26, 28, 31, 32, 33, 34, 41, 43, 44, 45, 47
waste management, 9, 21
waste treatment, 15, 22
waste water, 19
Websites, 52